Call from Paris

ALSO BY PRARTHO SERENO

Causing a Stir: The Secret Lives & Loves
  of Kitchen Utensils
  A book of poems illustrated by the
  author; Mansarovar Press, 2007

Garden Sutra
  A chapbook of poems; Finishing Line Press,
  2005

Everyday Miracles: An A to Z Guide to the
  Simple Wonders of Life
  Essays; Kensington, 1998 (Published
  under the single name Prartho)

10/24/2018

Call from Paris

Prartho Sereno

Winner of the **2007**
Washington Prize

THE WORD WORKS
WASHINGTON, D.C.

Acknowledgments

Grateful acknowledgment is made to the following publications in
which some of these poems first appeared:

JOURNALS:

Atlanta Review: "Call from Paris," "Explorations of a Heart in Space,"
"Sestina for the Gypsy's Daughters" (International Publication
Prize, 2004), "Fish" (International Publication Prize, 2005)

Branches: "Werner Was Right" (Pushcart Nomination)

Chautauqua Literary Journal: "Love in the Time of War"

Comstock Review: "Ode to Tears," "Fallen," "Swallowing the World"
(Poem of Special Merit, 2004)

Drumvoices Revue: "10,000 Names for Rain"

Lucid Stone: "The Man Who Stopped Eating in January"

Oxalis: "One Last Sadness" (Special Award in Poetry, 1991)

Poetry Motel: "Monsoon Mud"

Rattle: "Love of Distance"

Runes: "Music of the Spheres" (formerly, "Flying Home")

Viha Connection (International Meditation Journal)*:* "Blind Night
Running," "Garden Sutra"

White Pelican Review: "Borderlands"

ANTHOLOGIES:

Finding Marin: Stories of Home: "Living on 4th Street"

Heart Flip (California Poets in the Schools 2001 Anthology): "Spell"

Ithaca Women's Anthology: "Teatime with Nisha"

In the Company of Women: "Shaman," "Noah's Wife and the Change
of Life"

Marin Poetry Center Anthology 2001: "Shaman," "First Frost,"
"Mariam"

Moon Won't Leave Me Alone (2003 CPITS Anthology): "Juvenile Hall"

Pieces of Our Lives: "Setting Back the Clocks"

Still Going Strong: "Noah's Wife and the Change of Life," "If Love
Comes to Me Again"

The Gift of Experience (*Atlanta Review* 10th Anniversary): "Call from
Paris"

CHAPBOOK:
Some of these poems appeared in the chapbook
        Garden Sutra; Finishing Line Press,
        Georgetown, Kentucky, 2005.

        I'd also like to thank my loyal writing partners,
        Bill Keener & Mike Day; the Marin Arts Council;
        California Poets in the Schools; and my students,
        fellow teachers, friends, and family for their generous
        support.

for Dennis

So instead of giving way to this homesickness,
I said to myself: that land . . . is everywhere.

—Vincent van Gogh
in a letter to his brother Theo

Contents

Part III

Part IV

PART

Song

When the soul gets homesick
she goes back to when she was cut
from the hide of night, back
before the Word, when she hung
in utter silence on the moist roof
of the cave's mouth.

She reassumes the otherworldly
shape, sleeps upside-down
and wakes with the disappearing light.
When the others have bowed their heads
and folded in their feathers,
she shakes herself and flies.

Leather-winged and blind, she cries out
until the landscape enters her like a song,
the sound of her own voice gathering
into points of light. And then she remembers
how the dark pelt from which she was taken
teemed with stars.

Spell

Before the alphabet was snatched up
by the mind, it belonged to the body.
Consonants huddled in the crooks of
elbow, ankle and knee, where they thrived
on gossip and potluck dinners,
built cities with jazz clubs and intricate
webs of phone-line and highway.

But the vowels, moon-driven and drunk
on the sound of their own voices,
lived alone in the hollows and caves.

O, the Emperor of Solitude,
built his hut in the dome of the belly.
With wingspan and vision of an eagle,
I made his nest in the brows.
U, the hermit thrush, hid her rubies
in the isthmus of the throat. And the lioness
E staked claims on the mouth,
raising her cubs on intermittent light.

But it was *A*, wild and lovely,
who holed up in the heart.
Caught in the spell of *ah* . . .
in the *ah* of awaiting, of awkward
and aflame. In the nearly inaudible *ah*
of being folded into the arms
of the lover without a face.

Calling

Some are called at an early age,
learn the way one aimless step leads
to another and the waist-deep fields
of summer part for the urchin child.

The way something bright and shadow-
flecked floats in on the scent of clover,
enters the body and lingers there.
Hidden among the sumac at the edge

of the road, even the clamoring child
can be overcome by stillness,
turn suddenly old and silent—
a moss-covered entrance to the ruins.

Sometimes they came looking for me—my mother
ringing the cowbell, my brothers' panicked footfalls
like wingbeats along the ridge. Their voices
braided through me like a river.

Garden Sutra

When the disciple is ready, the master appears.
In extreme cases, disguised as a garden—
overgrown, inherited from a previous tenant

with a passion for wild vines and grasses
that spread until everything is lost in one
spectacular tangle, a few pale blossoms dangling

from exhausted stems. She thought of hiring
a gardener—one of the sturdy Guatemalans
who waited every morning near the on-ramp,

but she kept putting it off, consumed with digging
in the cool loam at the center of her chest, digging
for traces of what the Stranger planted there in the dark.

She was taken by the man in the *New Yorker* story
who went blind in his forties and slowly sank
into what he called deep blindness: the long slow

meltdown of inner images into cloudless sky.
She went with him all the way back to the clean
blank slate and its sudden unexpected turn,

the quick-change of engine for caboose, cause
for effect, so that life's train sped backward, the end
of every story becoming the way it begins.

That's when she saw it was the flutter of sycamore leaves
that invited the wind, the sky's turn to indigo and
the air's slow cooling that released the sun to set.

The late-summer dahlias were what called her hands,
wrist-deep, into June's jungle of roots.
Because the delphiniums were soul-searing blue,

she dug a hole. Because she was overcome
with joy, he loved her like no one else. Because
she was drenched with loss, he disappeared.

Time, Somewhere

Somewhere time is still
as huge as it was when we rocked
in the soot of the old Franklin,
baked bread, put up apple butter,
mended holes in pockets and socks.

As huge as when you and I stood
at the iced pane, tracing the low-
slung arc of the sun with our fingers.

Somewhere time still swells and ebbs
with the moon, still harbors
the sunken jewels and wails
her mournful madrigals. But we
don't hear them anymore.

Sometimes I think she's been caught
by the fisherman who trawls the skies
in his skiff called dusk.

Sometimes I think I see her
rolling in his phosphorescent nets:
Mother of Stillness, Queen
of the Low Note, Guardian of Things
Beyond Our Eyes. Sometimes I hear
her humming to you—humming

the tune with which she brought you
from the depths, swaddled in light,
into the relentless ticking of the world.

Death and Fortune Cookies

i.   Whenever she cuts your hair, strands
dropping to the floor, she jokes,
Even if a woman has wandered barefoot
fifty years on Philippine sand,
the first gift from her Norwegian husband
will be a snow hat and ski boots.
Her face drifts behind you in the mirror,
a burnished saffron moon.
It's the sultry island air, she confides,
that keeps us looking so young.

But in June, when you ask for her
at the shop, the owner struggles
to look up. And when he finally does,
his gaze and words fall through you,
as if your body has become a rabbit hole
where death hops in.

Yes, that is exactly what enters you—death,
with its ammonia smell and metallic
rounds of chemotherapy, polishing
the mirror without her face.

ii.   Later that week, life returns in the shape
of twin grandsons, come to summer with you.
In the first days, one muses out the car window,
I love everything about falling—except one.
And when you ask which one, he says,
Hitting the ground.
But the rest I love . . . the breeze . . .
The surprise! his brother calls from the back seat.
The feeling of flying! Yes, they sing
in their inimitable harmony: *The feeling of flying.*

18

You won't remember this as you fall through
the month of July, surrender your living room
to dirty socks, seagull bones and ocean rocks,
your teakettle to a colony of pollywogs.
Give yourself to watching—puppet shows
and flips into the swimming hole, a gaggle
of dances: the Harlem Shake, the Crypt Walk,
and one where they dust each other off,
called the Friend.

You won't notice your hair turning silver
like a poplar taken by a sudden wind.
Or how, at the Chinese restaurant, you reach
with unusual hunger for your fortune.

iii. On the drive to the airport, the boys
will whistle and whoop their good-byes
to the landmarks and neighbors.
*You don't mind if we yell
out the windows today,* says one.
Then the other: *Because you want our voices
to ring in your ears.* And it will be true,
because you know you will soon
be hitting the ground. Nothing left
but the ring of those voices and the crumpled
strips of paper in your pocket—a cookie baker
in Chinatown assuring you, *You will step
on the soil of many countries,* and,
*The most difficult things in life
are not always the most important.*

What I Brought from India
for my Brother Greg

Seven years of water
had gone down the Ganges
before I came to you again—
in the rain, empty-handed as ever
with my two kids and a mountain
of duffel bags on the train platform
on Easter Sunday in the dark.
I asked myself how I could
show you these eyes that hold
less and less when I so wanted
to bring you something: a map,
a tapestry, a wonderful story,
and not the only thing I have,
which is a little bit of nothing,
a space inside the jungle
where the silence sits
and sings its strange song.
I've found that whatever
I've found in my life
is no good to anyone,
except perhaps as a nudging
elbow into the ribs of the reticent
angel that she might whisper:
Go on, go on, into your own
deepest hopes and find—
or lose—whatever you can.

Monsoon Mud

monsoon mud
is very forgiving
she does not hold
the footprint long

Blue Mosque

That place we dropped into
last night, each from our own sky,
into Istanbul's yellow lamp-light,
into the windless eye.

Into the place where love lays
himself against the cliff, like the friend
who so many years ago clung
to the fence posts and unrolled his body
letting me climb his rungs
of ankle, knee, sacrum, rib.

Love laid himself down like that.

In the morning, mortal again,
shuffling alongside the crowd and their cameras,
carrying our shoes in plastic bags,
we wandered onto the prayer rugs—
hundreds of them, end to end
and golden under the great bowl.
Above us in the ethers,
motes of dust, lit and turning . . .

On my knees again and weeping.
Not prepared to drop like this,
so helpless or so soon.

Back to where we were
in last night's chambers,
somewhere deep inside me.
Or is that dome of silence
and light inside you?

Blind Night Running

Early this morning friends tell you
she fell asleep at the wheel
and tumbled out of her body,
and through the hole this leaves

in you, the Transparent One
slips inside again, urges:
Come quickly now;
we travel only in darkness
and our nights grow short.

It doesn't matter anymore
what you do in the light,
only that you give yourself
to this blind night running.

Rampant or lazy, buoyant
or weeping, alone
or in company; nothing counts now,
but your blazing body
burning its way home.

Into White

At the far end of each of these lines you will be asked
to jump. From every end-word you will sail out
only to flap your way back to fresh outcroppings
of symbol and sound. This is what you signed on for
when you turned the page—this sigh and scramble
over black needles and ravines, every breath drawing
you deeper into the clean white page. Listen as it laps
against us as we speak. O but how eagerly we claw
our way back to this dark spine of words . . . Until
the inevitable swallows us, which it soon enough will,
Dear Reader, for the time has come to gather yourself;
to discover at last what the suicide-jumper finds
on his way down: Every problem could have been solved
but this.

PART

Slow-Motion Mambo

For our next spin round the sun
let's bring down the tempo,
commit ourselves to a slow sauté
of shuffle, swoop, and glide.

Let's fall in with the polar bear's lumber,
the newt's wobble,
the sea turtle's heavy-lidded blink.

We will devote entire days
to sweeping the walk; give way
to beetles as they cross,
to leaves as they color and fall.

Let's tune ourselves to the wind harp,
shake out the sheets till they're fragrant
with jasmine, string up a hammock
under the blossoms and not get up
till the peaches are ripe.

Let's take back roads home,
moonwalk the children to school,
cobble a life of gaze and hum
and back-stoop story.

We'll stop saving time and spend it—
lob in the towel and freefall through honey.

We will learn to wait till the mountains
bow down and the rivers come home.
Until the lines of our bodies are almost
erased, so that light wanders through us
as if we were Saturday morning.

Borderlands

Once she drove taxi on graveyard shift
for a remote town in the Oregon desert,
the salt rush of night her only tide.
She came to know the coyote's call, his silver

body in moonlight. She came to know
the valley of shooting stars, where deer
wandered on delicate legs far from fear.
She learned how the membranes of things

dissolved in the dark, how she could
hold the beasts and comets inside her
when no one was looking. And in the darkest hour
when the Earth was sated with sleep

she learned how the sun would rise
like a pitcher and fill things back up
so the edges were taut, resolute—
an effect so convincing even she believed again

in boundaries, even as her heart
veered back toward the borderlands
with their steamy songs, their dance halls
strung with colored lights.

10,000 Names for Rain

Today a little rain—nothing
so extravagant as the great sheets
she hangs out along the cliffs
of Lake Ontario, but what you
who grew up inside the lake effect
called *drizzle*.

Yet even as the word
hums in your mouth, you feel
the poverty of your tongue.
Where you come from
there were never enough names
for the songs the sad
gray lady sang.

And so from inside your car
outside the laundromat,
you resolve to begin
the tedious chore of naming:

You will call this rain *Soft
and Steady on the Steel Blue Roof.*
You will call it *The Mourners
Who Left for the Mountains, The Song of Missing Him,
The Bringing Down of Summer Leaves.*

You will call it *The Smell
of Pine Trees, Glass Wind Chimes at the End
of the Hall, The Memory of Mr. Porreca
Fishing in His Raincoat.* You will call it *The Sound
of Cornflowers Weeping in a Jar,
The Whoosh of Walking through Sand.*

You will call it *What the Sun
Will Never Know*—middle child
of *The Empty Gourd* and
The Old Woman's Secret Sorrow.

Music of the Spheres

He's finally stopped,
the boy in droopy socks
and runny nose,
stretched-out sleeves
of his sweater flapping
like dilapidated wings.
The one who between
Bombay and Singapore
moaned and writhed
in the aisle
like a rain cloud.

He broke when we
lifted off from Seoul,
drenching us in sobs
until we were beside
ourselves, watching him
stagger under his squalls
of grief. But now,
suspended over
the dark Pacific,
he falls still.

His father is peeling
an orange, holding it up
in the solitary reading lamp,
where it glows like a planet
not yet named—a radiant world
the father breaks open
and divides between
himself and the boy,
one glistening section
at a time.

Teatime with Nisha

Half-past ten and my *Flying Camel*
Cleaning partner falls into the sofa,
her blue eyes ablaze, like jewels.
Now vee sit, she says,
passing on tea, launching
into story. *These days cleaning*
bring it all back, every hair
of my flea-bitten life.

And she takes me down the wet
cobbled post-war streets
into the clapboard house—
kids all over, pots on the stove,
the burden of an afternoon that stays
beyond all decency.
But the husband appears
in the doorway, flowers
and wine in his rough hand.
The lovelight of his face.

We return, her sapphires
smoldering underwater.
Sometimes I vant it back!
She grabs a piece of air
and squeezes it. *I vant my life back.*
And her fierceness melts into laughter,
into the couch, into the room.
The whole world goes soft
and gives back her life.

Living in India

This morning it's sadness again,
standing at my door like a farmer
smelling of the earth—gentle

and persistent, handing me
the trowel. He is asking me
to work the soil of my grief.

I was hoping for someone else,
like the *dhobi* collecting laundry,
or a woman with a basket of fruit on her head.

But you are an old friend.
Come, sit, and have a little breakfast
on the slate bench in my garden.

The birds aren't afraid of you,
they'll come to eat the crumbs.

Living on 4th Street

It is dangerous to have breakfast
by the picture window,
all the clocks muttering behind you.
Especially if the wind
has blown up her menagerie of leaves—
billowy, mud-colored creatures
at the edge of extinction.
And if the trash cans start to rattle
against the wispy drone.
And if all the faces of the morning
walkers disappear inside
their hooded coats.
Time has a way of getting up
and walking out on you.

Werner Was Right

Werner was right,
after the accident
nothing was the same.
The phone still rang
and everybody knew their lines.
But the birds sang
with greater urgency,
their bodies were lighter at liftoff,
and it felt as if someone
had turned off a radio
in the storeroom of her head.

The rain was wetter,
grass wilder and more green.
Her skull itched beneath the wound
like a memory trying to speak.

And she stopped wishing so hard
for life to go another way.

First Frost

What do we really know?
That which by habit we call
hard, this morning
looks so soft:

leaves rimmed in crystal,
gray silk parachute of a sky,
the white lies of our breath
disappearing between us.

Ode to Tears

There are no
differences
between tears;
I have tasted them
in all seasons
under all phases
of the moon,
and they all
taste of salt.

PART

Love in the Time of War

The last time we made love
the sadness of the world
got into me—a congregation
of fatherless boys, dangling
their legs from the broken
verandahs behind my eyes.
Evening coming on, and cooking fires—
a handful of fallen, eroded stars.
Nearly all the camels had died,
taken by a mysterious disease.
The streets were powdered
with broken bricks; everything
useful had been carted away.
And there was my brother
with a paintbrush at the back
of his house, telling me how
he'd never known loneliness,
really. But his gaze dropped
into the paint. Then he looked up
and said, *Maybe I did last night—*
when she walked out with the laundry.
And, as if on cue, the others
filed in—dark-eyed women
cloaked in children,
gunslingers bent in grief,
my mother's orphaned heart
and my father's hopeless love
of fixing things. The last time
we made love they all came through:
everything that leaps or lights.
Everything that dies. Even
our answered prayers—a flock
of bird-shaped clouds now
in a bright sky, dispersing.

Swallowing the World

My father is in the kitchen,
fluorescent halo on the ceiling,
night's face pressed against the window.
He is eating peanut butter on wheat
crackers and will eat the whole box,
the whole jar, before morning
when he will rise to put on
his herringbone suit and red
fleur-de-lis tie, go with us
to the church to be baptized.
My mother will be beside herself
with joy to see him enter the fold,
bottomless flannel pocket
of forgiveness and sin.

This is the scene I will take with me
into the badlands of adulthood,
not the next morning with its incense
and holy water, my mother
in a pillbox hat and tears, but
the peanut butter and crackers,
flickering tube of light, look of uncertain
trouble on my father's face.
I will carry this scene like an ache,
like a witch's bag of stones and bones.
I will carry it like a puzzle,
like a begging bowl. Like a koan.

I will go forth and live low
to the ground, crawl out
of my skin whenever I can.
I will learn to be still and listen
with my belly, to enter the long

space between winter breaths.
I will not trust the dark urgencies
that flap and dart from pulpits,
but the arias of hunger and thirst.
Anything I eat, I will swallow whole.
I will sleep in the arroyo for years,
wake up ravenous for light.

Walking Backward

Nobody knows what to say—
Earth on her knees, face deep
in the grotto of her hands—
but some are sent to wander, carry
the empty buckets and walk
backward like sacred lunatics.
Unlearn the words. Return
to the vacant field before the dream
was made solid and dazzling
with its reflective glass.

It's a strange assignment in a
god-hungry, aching world.
The bearers themselves worry
if they've got it right, but
press on, something clear
working its way through
the cracks—spring-waters
of silence, trust in what
can't be known—curatives
of the once and future king.

Juvenile Hall

Giovanni is not in poetry class today.
He's in lock-up, chants my wayward
Greek chorus, and for a moment
he's conjured up out of the hole,
standing there in his orange sweats,
all seventeen years, six and a half feet of him.
Cockeyed grin, incandescent globe of hair,
hands dangling like shoes
tossed over a telephone wire.
Funny how the freedom riders
always gallop full-steam into lock-up.
The ones whose poetry we love,
who can turn the sky into rainbow trout,
serve it up with a hot sauce of snow.
Funny how his presence tastes more like wind
than a room with no mattress
or windows.
More like a gust of laughter
so sweet and clear, even the guards
close their eyes to hear.

Salt

This much I know: I turn with her
in every telling, Lot's wife and I
in our nightgowns, straw sandals
clapping at our heels. God of our
childhood spitting at our backs.
Devouring what he has made—
trees and flowers, sheep and dogs.
Cows, chickens, children.

Above us a cold sky—blinding
in its pitch-dark radiance.
The men are strangely at home here,
running into the emptiness that knows
them by name. Their lungs drink deep.
The muscles of their thighs rejoice
as they leap. The sky parts as if
in answer to their towers and spires,
what they hoped to touch each time
they entered us.

But Lot's wife and I are drawn, as always
by gravity. Our branching souls seep
into the teeming earth where we mingle
with the unthinkable, eat light and grow green.
Half of us is hidden—a musty tangle of want
mining the depths where all are blind, yet
everything courses inexplicably toward water.

How could Lot know of this? Why
she spent so much of herself in the garden,
burrowing among beetles and larvae,
flinging endless buckets of water.
All he knew was that she was his earth,

his food. He knew when they stopped running
she'd plant again. There would be olive trees
and date-palms, a backyard explosion of lavender.

Her shrine of muddy shoes and rake
would frame the door. The kitchen would be
steamy and fragrant with rosemary and garlic.
There would be goldfish in the pond.
Cooking spoons, embroidery floss, grandchildren.

She was not ignorant of what was required.
Simple enough: Don't look back.
Their god was always making rules like this,
with their dire consequences. Bite into an apple
and your children's children's children
will walk through the valley in the shadow of death.

He was a god of specifications and riddles,
seemed to have forgotten everything
about peat moss and gravel, humus and clay.
She forgave him this and meant to follow,
but a tendril caught her ankle and it all rushed back:
the barefoot boys of Gomorrah, their mothers
hanging out clothes, elders teetering beneath
bundles of wood. She saw the streets at dusk
when the coolness lifted everyone, without preference.

She was part of everything again, coming up
as pomegranate and wheat, the bright
palm leaves of her hands. She was sand grouse
and pipit. Broomstick and windowsill.
She was wind; she was fire.

She was a sunflower turning
its face toward its own larger self.

And in a breath, she was salt. A pillar—
exquisitely beautiful, translucent and still.

Lot went on. He did not look back,
but pushed deeper down the corridors
of night, leaving his wife to be windswept
and broken. Dispersed. Sent back
to live among us. To be poured into jars.
To be tasted on our lips. And to fall
into the ordinary glory of our days.

Shaman

I've been trying a long time
to write the poem about you
as shaman, one who arrives
ready to die, only to rise
from the ashes again
and again. About finding
you on the porch steps
at the age of three, kicking
the backboard like a drum,
your pupils the shapes of hawks.
The other mothers were
teaching the alphabet; not
that I didn't try, but mostly
I stepped back, kept
a quiet circle around you
in the woods and fields.
In time, the wing beats
in your chest grew louder.
You were not easy to watch;
wherever you smelled death
you walked in. Running
away from home in a midnight
blizzard, sleeping in a tree house
with the street people, giving
birth to twins at seventeen.
You cannot see it yet,
but one day you will know
why you had to walk such thorny ground.
A weathered shaman will reveal herself
from beneath your youth mask.
She will walk through rooms thick
with fear, dry the tears of the weeping,
make the frozen ones laugh.

Noah's Wife and the Change of Life

No one ever talks about
what happens to Noah's wife
after the boat lands.

Her life on the ark is no secret—
day in and out adrift in that
wooden pod oozing with musk,
all manner of lovers
all over the place.
Long necks, curling feathers,
and those terribly innocent eyes.

What happens to Noah's wife
when the rain stops and the dove
returns, olive branch in her mouth,
when the boat sighs and settles
on a sun-baked rock?

I'll tell you: she leaves.
She wakes up one day
and can no longer live
with the smell of her past.
She gets up and walks
into the newly hatched
mountains and there
she joyfully loses herself.

Fallen

Some say she flew so close
that her wings flared up,
went to pieces, turned to ash,
and that's how she fell
back down to the world.
But I know different.

I've seen her in pawnshops
trading her magic, feather
by feather, lugging home
odd-shaped artifacts, things
of substance and weight, stuff
that aches with hope:
Persian carpets, silver parrot
on a string, and books
with songbirds on their covers,
their ornate cages swinging
in dappled light.
I've heard her at dusk
calling for the dark, smelled
the night jasmine growing thick
and tangled outside her door.

The truth is, she's lost by choice.
Happy, like Jonah, in the belly
of her whale, where she sings of swans
and flying fish, gliding lizards
and luna moths, sings to the world
that turns inside her,
its dark night full of wings.

Man Overboard

When he looks up from his beer
and asks her if she's living
the life she wants to be living,
she sees by the color of his eyes
he is sinking.

And like a piece of driftwood,
she tosses out, *My life comes closer
than I thought it would . . .*

But on their way out of the bar,
he points to the blue world
inside the TV and murmurs,
Submarine movie, with a translucent
sigh, and she knows
he's going down for the third time.

Later, in her flat, he dives into her,
the urgency of a drowning man,
leaves her sculling the waves
in bobbing candlelight
and moaning *shakuhachi* flute.

And next day she finds
the pearl of sadness he left in her,
a tiny moon she can carry
in the palm of her hand,
made from a grain
of their happiest day.

The Man Who Stopped Eating in January

i.   January echoes like the hollow
at the edge of your land,
where the timid creatures
come to drink, and the sound
of someone breathing
can fill the whole night.

It is here, in this snowy basin,
that the man in tune
with the rites of wintering
at last refuses to eat.

ii.   Closing that door, deciding
not to swallow anything
anymore, softer moments
bubble up. Like his telling you
over the phone, when this is all over
he's coming for a visit.

You know in this world
where the telephone rests
on your ear and the cat
is out stalking rabbits,
there will be no visit.

But in the world the other
is leaning toward, perhaps
the promise can be kept.

iii.   He will walk lightly
without the old baggage: a body

that spent itself wandering
more than eighty years
through New York's straight-edged
mazes, desperately seeking roundness,
taking comfort in the smells
that collect in the overturned bowls
of bypasses and bridges.

Unburdened
he will simply take the shape
of the space between the trees,
he will be clothed in the songs
of a hundred morning birds,
his stomach will not ache.

iv.   And though the soul cannot stand
in the world where phone lines run,
cats stalk, and pages turn,
you will know when he has come,
because you who can catch
stardust as it sifts down
through the sky will always know
the emperor, whether or not
he arrives in clothes.

And because the man
who could lift you to the ceiling
as you stood in his hands
has always trusted what you
yourself can never see.

Sestina for the Gypsy's Daughters

When the girl who sat next to me, so good on the parallel bars,
vanished in the middle of the school year, word rushed
through the halls she'd left for the circus, just like in the stories,
but this time for real. Her glittering trapeze-artist family
walked out on the tarnished world, and my heart went with them,
hung beneath the Big Top, so my teachers had to pluck me
       from the air.

It was good I had girls. Years later when the marriage burst
       into thin air,
it was good I had girls, with their easy laughter and chocolate-bar
eyes. When their dreams came unraveled, I could sing to them.
When their shiny new lunch pails looked foolish, I could rush,
heroine in hoop earrings, turn them dull & old. It ran in the
       family—
my father could turn buttons to coins, tears to stories.

It was good I had girls, content to eat flatbread and stories,
sew coins in the linings of their skirts, put on bracelets and airs.
Practice seeing through the veil into the broken-hearted family
of things. Read palms and tarot, lift the iron window bars
to reveal the swirling stars, and headlong rush
into the streets, a secret language between them.

They learned to pack deep and travel light—nothing to hold them.
To scatter good-byes and pull themselves up by the roots.
       Their story
was not catastrophic, just sad, as they bore the salt-water rush
of envy for all things that stayed put—houses with basements
       and attic air,
the net beneath the other girls' leaps, the tightrope walker's bar.
The only fortunes they couldn't tell were their own. It ran in
       the family.

All gypsy daughters feel like orphans in the great sturdy family,
riding an underground railroad of schools, no one to eat lunch
  with them.
Always the strange new girls, not even good on the parallel bars.
No one's hearts big enough to take in their stories.
No one waiting upside-down as they're flung into the air.
Wrapped in hand-dyed cloth they are sent to drift among the
  rushes.

But the river is kind. It embraces its pilgrims and never rushes.
Takes them the long way home—through every color of family
into regions where orphans are treasures they lift into the air.
I watch as it takes them downstream; no longer can I rock them
or assure them of the easy climb over the hilly lines and stories
of their hands. I still sing, but can they hear me through the
  bars?

And I still hang from the Big Top, far from the urge to rush,
  me or them—
our zigzag scramble from town to town just a ragged family story
on which to do our sequined magic: turn the air to music, a few
  simple bars.

One Last Sadness

I have so much water
inside me,
so many wild winds,
and more than enough salt.

Man of the sea,
I could have been
your ocean.

PART

IV

Call from Paris

Whistling down the wires
that string together the world,
your voice: *It never stops
raining here*, you say. *Paris
is an ocean of chatter and smoke,*

a sea of umbrellas. You tell me
the phone booth is a glass-bottom
boat, the Seine keeps flooding
her banks, and last night
at dinner you couldn't think

of a thing to say. You tell me
you are part of something
old now. You cannot believe
the way the sky opened
inside the cathedral, the way

the chants lifted you up
like a waterwheel, broke you
into a thousand shining pieces
and sent you raining
back to the world.

Mariam

The Swiss woman has a few teeth
missing, a nest of tiny twigs
around the eyes. *Nobody*
believes an old woman, she says,
flashing a falling-down fencepost
smile. *They think she is just crazy . . .*

But there are birds, she tells me,
that hardly come down from the sky at all.
Only to bear their young, she goes on
with those unblinking eyes.

They fly very high,
past a certain point
where gravity doesn't
count for much
and they hang there
and sleep
like fish sleep in the ocean.

Explorations of a Heart in Space

My wiz-kid brother tells me—eyes
flickering with dark matter and nebulae—
that if the earth were the size of a cue ball,

it would be smoother. Or conversely,
if a cue ball were blown up to the size
of the earth, its canyons would be grander,

its Himalayas higher. Now take your very
human heart (a cue ball would outsmooth it
in any contest), take your heart and expand it,

blow it up to the size of the earth,
to the size of the sun. Into what wonders
would its canyons open? Onto what peaks

could you climb? And if your longboat were
left to drift from her mother ship,
into what shimmering seas would you sail?

Thief

She's stealing time again—
idle in broad daylight,
in the arboretum with the languid

retired folk, those who earned
their leisure honestly, while she was busy
falling through the net of duties,

her life too liquid to be caught.
She is grateful, mind you,
otherwise she would not have found

the milky-eyed old man in the shivering
shade of the almond tree. And the radio,
which is cradled on his knee and tuned

to the violins and flutes of his breaking
heart, would not be singing to her now.

If Love Comes to Me Again

If love comes to me again
as a man with dark eyes,
and if he says to me
Open . . .
If he reaches for me
when I am afraid,
turns my face to his
and asks, *Why hold back?*
Maybe someday I'll decide
you're not my type. Couldn't
you love yourself through that?
Perhaps I will think, *I know things*
now I didn't know then.
But love, in his tall hat
and lanky arms, in his infinite
pursuit of me, will wipe out
the lie called memory
in a single glance.

Love of Distance

He's enchanted with the idea
of reaching through space,
wants me to wait by the window
while he climbs the far-off mountain,
sets up the light, flashes something back
in Morse code. He says we should begin
studying our dots and dashes, along with
smoke signals, the extravagantly long rolled *r*'s
of Spanish. Hand gestures of the deaf.

Or we could take the rim trail,
one of us staying on the southern lip
while the other heads north till our bodies
shrink to the size of tree-frogs. Then we can converse
across the canyon without effort, no need
to raise our voices. He is certain this will work,
that the atmosphere at these heights
will bear our words with a clarity
as yet unknown to us.

My faith in these things is weaker.
I dare not tell him the Far-Eastern stories—
the one where the poet builds two houses
on opposite shores of the lake. Gives one
to his sweetheart, who he tells to go in,
take up dulcimer or needlework, learn to love
the lonely ways. *Think of the surprise,*
he says. *One of our faces suddenly shining*
between the blackbirds and reeds.

What Summers Bring

One year it was grasshoppers.
A footfall on the path would lift them
sizzling with hope from the dry grass.
That was the year I learned the art
of hurling myself at a moment's notice,
sailing on air, knees ticking.
The art of starting again
and again from new ground.

Then there was the seacoast year
with its lentil soup and cinnamon tea.
And the thought-ridden man
who lit the stove and mumbled
salty words into the pot. The year
we watched dozens of wrought iron
headboards and gates grow into antiques
in the neighbor's yard, our own
hinges rusting alongside.

But this was the summer of river rocks
and fireflies, of setting myself out
like a wide-mouthed jar, waiting
for spark. The year my childhood
rippled back, as the boys skipped
their stones and light began
to inch toward me again—
hundreds of tiny eyes
blinking between the blackberries
at the edge of my life.

Setting Back the Clocks

Now that we've folded the day
back toward morning, the sun will set
on us mid-sentence, we'll roll out the streets
of our dreams with the dish suds.
We'll drift again in our winter teacups—
the world a smaller, darker place.

We'll string our rooftops with lights,
build fires in wood stoves, light candles,
tell stories—elastic and loose again,
all the words the abridgers took out
put back.
And we will sing.

All through the night you'll hear us—
with babes in arms and dogs at foot,
after dinner with Armagnac, around
the hearth with harmonica and sarod.
Out of the mother's deepest night,
her ruby-throated urchins will rise and sing.

The Happiest Thing

The happiest thing is morning,
just before you remember
who you are. Or,
the happiest thing is nightfall,
its deafening of the eye
and dilation of the ear.

Happiest are the falling things—embers
from a burning log, water from a pitcher.
The dropped struggle, the sleepy body,
a long, hard rain.

Or, happiest are the lifted ones—
fountain pen and toothbrush,
an old banjo freshly strung.
A glass teacup, its eddies
of earth tone and steam.

No, happiest is the child
in worn-out sneakers sliding
on the frozen creek and hearing an echo
for the first time—mad for the voices
of those strange little people,
running into the woods to find them,
arms spread and flapping.

Yellow Bird

The day comes when you find yourself
on the train platform, deep space of India around you.
The grief and squawks from the rafters too much
for the yellow bird that is your heart—she opens herself
      and flies.

On the train platform, deep space of India around you,
a storm of dust and feathers rains down,
for the yellow bird you carried has opened herself and flown.
High in the rafters, she weaves her boat of silver thread.

A storm of dust and feathers rains down,
the conductor is calling for you to board.
High in the rafters she weaves her boat, leaves you
with an empty nest at the center of things.

The conductor is calling for you to board.
Who could have dreamed life would give this much?
An empty nest at the center of things, lined
like the one that fell in your garden, with your own hair.

Who could have dreamed life would give this much
silver thread with which to weave a listening seat?
Like the nest that fell in your garden, made of your own hair,
where you sit and listen for her return. Years and years.

All this silver thread with which to weave a listening seat,
stars to count, feathers to bead and string.
You sit and listen for her return. Years and years,
with closed eyes and the smell of the red clay floor.

Stars to count, feathers to bead and string,
the grief and squawks from the rafters too much.
With closed eyes and the smell of the red clay floor,
the day comes when you find yourself.

Fish

We have to do our part, it seems—
make small, but whole-hearted gestures;
fling, for example, thin silver offerings
in arcs over the water so they glint
against the sky like dragonflies.

Young boys catch on quickest;
with the day swimming through them
by breakfast their laps are full
of bluegill and perch.

My friend Bodhi casts his line into the mirror
each morning: *How come you ain't happy?*
he croons to the fish in the glass. He knows
how unexpectedly grace can leap from the water,
how entranced grace is with our rarefied air and light.

Coleridge kept his hatches unbattened
so the depth-dwellers would slither in and out—
strange primordial creatures transparent as glass,
phosphorescent skeletons flickering
in the murk. Maybe he knew

that every gesture is a prayer,
and every prayer is answered.
And every answer is a fish.
That's why we see them circling over death-beds:

Rabindranath shouting at the Brahmin priest,
who prays that the poet be freed from the wheel
of birth and death: *Stop all this nonsense!*
Tell God I want *His earth and His seas.*
Tell Him I'm hungry for fish!

And Gertrude Stein grasping at the last
straws: *What is the answer?* she warbles,
but then shakes her head and laughs:
All those years of hook, line, and sinker . . .
and it turns out I am the fish!

For the Drifters

They say the continents are still drifting,
nudged each year a little further into the blue.
And through the sand and waterways drift
the herds—goat tribes and ant colonies,
pods of whales and knots of toads.

For millennia dust has drifted in and out of
doorways, and in their seasons, pollen and snow.
It turns out even glass drifts. The vertical
panes that hold our world in place are more
like sheets of rain than walls, their bottoms
growing thicker down the years.

The truth is, we are all leaning on water.
But some of us lean harder, deeper. This poem
is for you—the fallen, with limbs worn to silk.
For you light-footed ones, tramped on in the fray.
This poem is for all of you solitary singers,
adrift in the great dark ship of your song.

About the Author

PRARTHO SERENO is author of a chapbook of poems, *Garden Sutra*; a book of essays, *Everyday Miracles: An A to Z Guide to the Simple Wonders of Life*; and author/illustrator of a book of illuminated poems, *Causing a Stir: The Secret Lives & Loves of Kitchen Utensils*. She received a Marin Arts Council Individual Artist Grant for poetry in 2003. Her poems have appeared in such journals as *Atlanta Review*, *Chautauqua Review, Comstock Review, Runes, Rattle*, and *White Pelican Review*, and have been anthologized in various collections.

Photo by Angelina Sereno

A poet-teacher with California Poets in the Schools, she was awarded a 2005 Radio Disney Super Teacher Award. Sereno is a watercolor artist whose work has been chosen for book covers, such as *In the Company of Women* and *Pieces of Our Lives*, both edited by Trish Schiesser. She also dabbles in songwriting and produced her own song/music/poetry CD, *Salt*. She lives a little north of the Golden Gate Bridge with a sweet man and his cat.

About the Washington Prize

CALL FROM PARIS is the winner of the 2007 WORD WORKS Washington Prize. Prartho Sereno's manuscript was selected from among 257 manuscripts submitted by American poets.

FIRST READERS:

> Cliff Bernier, Doris Brody, Angelyn Donahue,
> W. Perry Epes, Michael Gushue, Erich Hintze,
> Tod Ibrahim, Sydney March, Mike McDermott,
> Ann Rayburn, Martha Sanchez-Lowery,
> Jill Tunick, and Doug Wilkinson

SECOND READERS:

> Mark Dawson, Brandon D. Johnson,
> and Judith McCombs

FINAL JUDGES:

> Karren L. Alenier, J. H. Beall, Bernadette Geyer,
> Miles David Moore, and Steven B. Rogers

About The Word Works

THE WORD WORKS, a nonprofit literary organization, publishes contemporary poetry in collectors' editions. Since 1981, the organization has sponsored the Washington Prize, a $1,500 award to an American poet. Monthly, The Word Works presents free literary programs in the Chevy Chase Café Muse series, and each summer, free poetry programs are held at the historic Joaquin Miller Cabin in Washington, DC's Rock Creek Park. Annually, two high school students debut in the Miller Cabin Series as winners of the Jacklyn Potter Young Poets Competition.

Since 1974, Word Works programs have included: "In the Shadow of the Capitol," a symposium and archival project on the African-American intellectual community in segregated Washington, DC; the Gunston Arts Center Poetry Series (Ai, Carolyn Forché, Stanley Kunitz, and others); the Poet-Editor panel discussions at the Bethesda Writer's Center (John Hollander, Maurice English, Anthony Hecht, Josephine Jacobsen, and others); and the Arts Retreat in Tuscany. Master Class workshops, an ongoing program, have featured Agha Shahid Ali, Thomas Lux, and Marilyn Nelson.

In 2008, The Word Works will have published 66 titles, including work from such authors as Deirdra Baldwin, J. H. Beall, Christopher Bursk, John Pauker, Edward Weismiller, and Mac Wellman. Currently, The Word Works publishes books and occasional anthologies under three imprints: the Washington Prize, the Hilary Tham Capital Collection, and International Editions.

Past grants have been awarded by the National Endowment for the Arts, National Endowment for the Humanities, DC Commission on the Arts & Humanities, Witter Bynner Foundation, Writer's Center, Bell Atlantic, Batir Foundation, and others, including many generous private patrons.

The Word Works has established an archive of artistic and administrative materials in the Washington Writing Archive housed in the George Washington University Gelman Library.

Please enclose a self-addressed, stamped envelope with inquiries.

THE WORD WORKS   PO Box 42164   Washington, DC 20015
    editor@wordworksdc.com   www.wordworksdc.com

WORD WORKS BOOKS

Karren L. Alenier, Hilary Tham, Miles David Moore, EDS.,
Winners: A Retrospective of the Washington Prize

* Nathalie F. Anderson, *Following Fred Astaire*

* Michael Atkinson, *One Hundred Children Waiting for a Train*

Mel Belin, *Flesh That Was Chrysalis* (HTC COLLECTION)

* Carrie Bennett, *biography of water*

* Peter Blair, *Last Heat*

Doris Brody, *Judging the Distance* (HTC COLLECTION)

Sarah Browning, *Whiskey in the Garden of Eden* (HTC COLLECTION)

Christopher Conlon, *Gilbert and Garbo in Love* (HTC COLLECTION)

Christopher Conlon, *Mary Falls* (HTC COLLECTION)

Donna Denizé, *Broken Like Job* (HTC COLLECTION)

Moshe Dor, Barbara Goldberg, Giora Leshem, EDS.,
The Stones Remember

James C. Hopkins, *Eight Pale Women* (HTC COLLECTION)

James C. Hopkins & Yoko Danno, *The Blue Door*
(INTERNATIONAL EDITIONS)

Brandon D. Johnson, *Love's Skin* (HTC COLLECTION)

Myong-Hee Kim, *Crow's Eye View: The Infamy of Lee Sang,
Korean Poet* (INTERNATIONAL EDITIONS)

Vladimir Levchev, *Black Book of the Endangered Species*
(INTERNATIONAL EDITIONS)

* Richard Lyons, *Fleur Carnivore*

* Fred Marchant, *Tipping Point*

Judith McCombs, *The Habit of Fire* (HTC COLLECTION)

* Ron Mohring, *Survivable World*

Miles David Moore, *The Bears of Paris* (HTC COLLECTION)

Miles David Moore, *Rollercoaster* (HTC COLLECTION)

Jacklyn Potter, Dwaine Rieves, Gary Stein, EDS.
Cabin Fever: Poets at Joaquin Miller's Cabin

* Jay Rogoff, *The Cutoff*

Robert Sargent, *Aspects of a Southern Story*

Robert Sargent, *A Woman From Memphis*

* Enid Shomer, *Stalking the Florida Panther*

* John Surowiecki, *The Hat City After Men Stopped Wearing Hats*

Maria Terrone, *The Bodies We Were Loaned* (HTC COLLECTION)

Hilary Tham, *Bad Names for Women* (HTC COLLECTION)

Hilary Tham, *Counting* (HTC COLLECTION)

Jonathan Vaile, *Blue Cowboy* (HTC COLLECTION)

* Miles Waggener, *Phoenix Suites*

Rosemary Winslow, *Green Bodies* (HTC COLLECTION)

* WASHINGTON PRIZE WINNERS